Closing Deals And Opening Doors
A Practical Guide to Real Estate Sales

NELLA BYRAN

Copyright

No part of this should be reproduced without the permission of the author.

© Nella Byran 2024

Contents

Introduction 4

Art of Real Estate Sales: An Overview 12

Understanding Your Market 16

The Sales Process: From Prospecting to Closing 20

Building Your Sales Arsenal 25

Effective Communication 30

The Psychology of Selling: Understanding Buyer Behavior 35

Creating Compelling Listings 40

The Open House Advantage 45

Negotiation Skills: Closing Deals with Confidence 49

Handling Objections: Turning Challenges into Opportunities 55

Technology in Sales: Leveraging Digital Tools for Efficiency 60

Networking and Relationship Building 66

Marketing Mastery 71

Time Management for Sales Professionals 77

The Closing Process: Sealing the Deal with Precision 83

Post-Sale Service: Building Client Loyalty and Referrals 88

Growing Your Real Estate Sales Career 93

Final thought 99

Introduction

Welcome to "Closing Deals and Opening Doors: A Practical Guide to Real Estate Sales," your essential companion on the journey to mastering the art of real estate sales. In the dynamic world of property transactions, success hinges not only on the ability to close deals but also on the skill to open doors to new opportunities. This book serves as your roadmap, guiding you through every step of the sales process and empowering you with the knowledge and techniques needed to thrive in this competitive industry.

The Art of Real Estate Sales is an intricate dance, blending market insight, communication finesse, and strategic negotiation. Our journey begins with an in-depth exploration of the foundational principles that underpin successful real estate sales. From understanding your market to mastering effective communication, each chapter is meticulously crafted to equip you with the tools and insights necessary to navigate the complexities of the industry with confidence and proficiency.

Understanding Your Market is key to unlocking the door to successful selling. We delve into the nuances of market dynamics, helping you decipher trends, identify opportunities, and tailor your approach to meet the ever-evolving needs of buyers and sellers. Armed with this knowledge, you'll be better equipped to position yourself as a trusted advisor and guide your clients toward their real estate goals.

The Sales Process is a journey, from prospecting to closing, filled with twists and turns. With a comprehensive roadmap at your disposal, you'll learn how to navigate each stage with precision and finesse. From building your sales arsenal to leveraging technology for efficiency, you'll discover practical strategies and techniques to streamline your workflow and enhance your effectiveness as a real estate professional.

Effective Communication lies at the heart of successful real estate sales. Whether you're engaging with clients, negotiating deals, or marketing properties, the ability to convey your message clearly and persuasively is paramount. In this section, we delve into the art of communication, exploring proven techniques to connect with clients, overcome objections, and forge lasting relationships built on trust and understanding.

The Psychology of Selling unveils the secrets behind buyer behavior, offering valuable insights into the motivations and desires that drive purchasing decisions. Armed with this understanding, you'll be better equipped to anticipate and address the needs of your clients, guiding them toward properties that resonate on both a practical and emotional level.

Creating Compelling Listings is an art form unto itself, requiring a delicate balance of creativity and strategic thinking. From crafting captivating property descriptions to showcasing homes in their best light, you'll learn how to create listings that capture the imagination of buyers and drive interest in your properties.

The Open House Advantage offers a powerful platform for showcasing properties and making lasting impressions. In this section, you'll discover strategies for planning and executing successful open houses that maximize exposure and generate excitement among potential buyers.

Negotiation Skills are essential for closing deals with confidence and finesse. Whether you're navigating price negotiations or addressing concerns raised by buyers or sellers, you'll learn how to approach each situation with poise and professionalism, securing favorable outcomes for your clients while preserving relationships and goodwill.

Handling Objections is a crucial skill for overcoming challenges and turning obstacles into opportunities. By understanding the underlying concerns driving objections, you'll be better equipped to address them effectively, fostering trust and confidence in your abilities as a real estate professional.

Technology in Sales has revolutionized the way we do business, offering powerful tools and resources to enhance efficiency and productivity. From customer relationship management systems to virtual tours and online marketing platforms, you'll learn how to leverage digital tools to streamline your workflow and amplify your impact in the marketplace.

Networking and Relationship Building are the cornerstones of long-term success in real estate sales. By cultivating meaningful connections and nurturing relationships with clients, colleagues, and industry partners, you'll create a powerful network that opens doors to new opportunities and fuels your growth as a professional.

Marketing Mastery is essential for promoting properties and attracting qualified buyers. In this section, you'll discover strategies for crafting compelling marketing campaigns that resonate with your target audience, driving interest and generating leads for your listings.

Time Management for Sales Professionals is key to maximizing productivity and achieving your goals. By implementing effective time management strategies and prioritizing tasks, you'll optimize your workflow and create space for growth and development in your real estate career.

The Closing Process marks the culmination of your efforts, as you seal the deal with precision and finesse. In this section, you'll learn how to navigate the intricacies of the closing process, ensuring a smooth and seamless transaction for all parties involved.

Post-Sale Service is essential for building client loyalty and generating referrals. By providing exceptional service and support after the sale, you'll foster lasting relationships with your clients and position yourself as their trusted advisor for future real estate needs.

Growing Your Real Estate Sales Career requires a long-term strategy and a commitment to continuous learning and improvement. In this final section, you'll discover strategies for advancing your career, expanding your skills, and achieving lasting success in the dynamic and rewarding world of real estate sales.

Whether you're a seasoned professional looking to sharpen your skills or a newcomer eager to make your mark, "Closing Deals and Opening Doors" is your comprehensive guide to real estate sales success. Packed with practical insights, actionable strategies, and real-world examples, this book will empower you to navigate the complexities of the industry with confidence and achieve your goals with clarity and conviction. So, let's embark on this journey together and unlock the door to your success in real estate sales.

Art of Real Estate Sales: An Overview

"The Art of Real Estate Sales: An Overview" serves as the foundational chapter in "Closing Deals and Opening Doors: A Practical Guide to Real Estate Sales." In this comprehensive overview, we delve into the fundamental principles and strategies that underpin successful real estate sales, setting the stage for your journey toward mastery in the field.

At its core, the art of real estate sales is about more than just transactions; it's about understanding the needs, desires, and aspirations of clients and guiding them toward their real estate goals with expertise and empathy. This chapter explores the multifaceted nature of the real estate sales profession, highlighting the blend of skills, knowledge, and personal qualities that contribute to success in the industry.

One of the key themes explored in this overview is the importance of building trust and credibility with clients. In a field where transactions involve significant financial and emotional investments, trust is paramount. We discuss strategies for establishing yourself as a trusted advisor, including transparent communication, ethical conduct, and a commitment to putting the client's interests first.

Another crucial aspect of the art of real estate sales is market intelligence. Successful sales professionals possess a deep understanding of market trends, local dynamics, and property values. By staying informed and attuned to changes in the market, you'll be better equipped to provide valuable insights and guidance to your clients, helping them make informed decisions about buying or selling property.

Effective communication lies at the heart of real estate salesmanship. Whether it's listening attentively to clients' needs, articulating the value of a property, or negotiating terms with other parties, strong communication skills are essential for building rapport, fostering understanding, and ultimately, closing deals. This chapter explores strategies for honing your communication skills and connecting with clients on a deeper level.

The art of real estate sales also encompasses the ability to navigate complex transactions with confidence and finesse. From conducting thorough property evaluations to negotiating terms and conditions, successful sales professionals possess a keen eye for detail and a strategic mindset. We discuss the importance of professionalism, integrity, and diligence in every aspect of the sales process, ensuring that transactions are conducted smoothly and ethically.

Finally, this overview emphasizes the importance of continuous learning and professional development in the field of real estate sales. The industry is constantly evolving, with new technologies, regulations, and market trends shaping the landscape. By staying curious, adaptable, and committed to growth, you'll position yourself for long-term success and relevance in a dynamic and competitive field.

In summary, "The Art of Real Estate Sales: An Overview" provides a comprehensive introduction to the core principles and strategies that underpin success in the field of real estate sales. By embracing the artistry of the profession—building trust, mastering market intelligence, honing communication skills, navigating transactions with finesse, and committing to lifelong learning—you'll be well-equipped to thrive in this rewarding and ever-changing industry.

Understanding Your Market

"Understanding Your Market: Keys to Successful Selling" is a pivotal chapter within "Closing Deals and Opening Doors: A Practical Guide to Real Estate Sales." Here, we embark on a journey deep into the intricacies of the real estate market, exploring the essential elements that drive successful selling and empower you to navigate the dynamic landscape with confidence and insight.

Central to this chapter is the recognition that each real estate market is unique, shaped by a complex interplay of factors such as geography, demographics, economic conditions, and local regulations. By gaining a comprehensive understanding of your specific market, you'll be better equipped to tailor your approach to meet the distinct needs and preferences of buyers and sellers within your area.

Market intelligence forms the bedrock of successful selling. We delve into the tools and techniques for gathering and analyzing market data, from tracking housing inventory and price trends to monitoring demographic shifts and economic indicators. By staying abreast of market dynamics, you'll be able to identify emerging opportunities, anticipate challenges, and adapt your strategies accordingly.

Key to successful selling is the ability to identify and leverage market trends. Whether it's a surge in demand for urban condominiums or a growing preference for sustainable, eco-friendly properties, understanding market trends allows you to position yourself as a trusted advisor, guiding clients toward properties that align with their preferences and investment goals.

Demographic analysis plays a crucial role in understanding market dynamics. By examining factors such as population growth, household income levels, and lifestyle preferences, you'll gain valuable insights into the evolving needs and preferences of potential buyers. Whether you're targeting first-time homebuyers, empty nesters, or investors, tailoring your marketing and sales approach to resonate with your target demographic is essential for success.

Economic conditions exert a significant influence on the real estate market. From interest rates and employment trends to consumer confidence and inflation rates, economic factors can impact housing demand, pricing dynamics, and overall market activity. By staying informed about macroeconomic trends and their implications for the local real estate market, you'll be better equipped to anticipate shifts and adjust your strategies accordingly.

Local regulations and zoning laws can also shape the real estate landscape, influencing property values, development opportunities, and investment potential. Understanding the regulatory environment in your market allows you to navigate potential obstacles and capitalize on opportunities in a compliant and ethical manner.

In summary, "Understanding Your Market: Keys to Successful Selling" equips you with the knowledge and insights needed to thrive in the complex and dynamic world of real estate sales. By gaining a deep understanding of your market's unique characteristics, trends, and dynamics, you'll be empowered to make informed decisions, provide valuable guidance to clients, and ultimately, achieve success in your real estate career.

The Sales Process: From Prospecting to Closing

"The Sales Process: From Prospecting to Closing" is a comprehensive chapter within "Closing Deals and Opening Doors: A Practical Guide to Real Estate Sales." In this chapter, we dissect the journey from initial prospecting to the final closing, exploring each step in detail and providing practical insights and strategies to navigate the sales process effectively.

Prospecting: The sales process begins with prospecting, the identification and cultivation of potential clients. This involves various strategies such as networking, cold calling, attending industry events, and leveraging online platforms. Effective prospecting is about building relationships and generating leads that have the potential to translate into successful transactions.

Qualifying Leads: Not all prospects are created equal. Qualifying leads involves assessing their readiness, motivation, and ability to buy or sell property. By asking probing questions and listening attentively to their needs and preferences, you can determine whether a lead is worth pursuing further or not.

Initial Contact and Needs Assessment: Once leads are qualified, the next step is to make initial contact and conduct a thorough needs assessment. This involves understanding the client's objectives, preferences, budgetary constraints, and timeline. By establishing clear lines of communication and demonstrating genuine interest in their goals, you lay the foundation for a productive and successful working relationship.

Property Search and Selection: Based on the client's needs and preferences, the next step is to conduct a targeted property search. This involves scouring listings, scheduling viewings, and presenting options that align with the client's criteria. By providing personalized recommendations and expert guidance, you help clients make informed decisions about potential properties.

Offer and Negotiation: Once a suitable property is identified, the next step is to prepare and present an offer to the seller. This involves crafting a compelling offer that reflects the client's interests while also negotiating terms and conditions that maximize their value. Effective negotiation requires a combination of market knowledge, strategic thinking, and excellent communication skills.

Contract and Due Diligence: Upon reaching an agreement with the seller, the next step is to finalize the contract and conduct due diligence. This involves reviewing legal documents, conducting property inspections, and addressing any contingencies or concerns that may arise. By ensuring transparency and thoroughness throughout the due diligence process, you minimize the risk of surprises or complications down the line.

Closing Preparation: As the closing date approaches, diligent preparation is essential to ensure a smooth and seamless transaction. This may involve coordinating with various parties involved in the transaction, such as lenders, attorneys, and inspectors, to ensure all necessary paperwork and requirements are met in a timely manner.

Closing: The culmination of the sales process is the closing, where ownership of the property is transferred from the seller to the buyer. This involves signing the final paperwork, exchanging funds, and completing any remaining tasks to officially seal the deal. By guiding clients through the closing process with professionalism and attention to detail, you ensure a positive and memorable experience for all parties involved.

Throughout each step of the sales process, effective communication, attention to detail, and a commitment to customer service are paramount. By understanding the nuances of the process and leveraging proven strategies and techniques, you can navigate the journey from prospecting to closing with confidence and success, ensuring positive outcomes for your clients and building a reputation as a trusted and reliable real estate professional.

Building Your Sales Arsenal

"Building Your Sales Arsenal: Tools and Techniques for Success" is a pivotal chapter within "Closing Deals and Opening Doors: A Practical Guide to Real Estate Sales." This chapter is dedicated to equipping you with the essential tools and techniques needed to excel in the competitive world of real estate sales. Let's explore in detail the key components of building your sales arsenal:

Customer Relationship Management (CRM) Systems: A CRM system is a powerful tool for managing client interactions, organizing leads, and tracking communication history. By centralizing client data and communication, CRM systems enable you to nurture relationships more effectively, follow up with leads in a timely manner, and stay organized throughout the sales process.

Property Management Software: Property management software streamlines tasks related to listing management, scheduling appointments, and tracking property data. These tools help you stay organized and efficient, allowing you to easily update listings, schedule showings, and manage client inquiries with ease.

Virtual Tours and 3D Imaging: Virtual tours and 3D imaging technologies allow prospective buyers to explore properties remotely, providing immersive experiences that showcase the features and layout of a property in vivid detail. By incorporating virtual tours into your marketing efforts, you can attract more qualified leads, save time on property showings, and differentiate yourself from competitors.

Social Media and Digital Marketing Platforms: Social media and digital marketing platforms offer powerful channels for reaching and engaging with potential clients. By leveraging platforms such as

Facebook, Instagram, and LinkedIn, you can amplify your reach, target specific demographics, and showcase properties to a wider audience. Additionally, email marketing campaigns and online advertising can help you stay top-of-mind with leads and drive traffic to your listings.

Data Analytics and Market Research Tools: Data analytics and market research tools provide valuable insights into market trends, pricing dynamics, and consumer behavior. By analyzing data on housing inventory, sales trends, and demographic shifts, you can make informed decisions about pricing strategies, target markets, and investment opportunities.

Presentation and Communication Tools: Presentation and communication tools, such as slide decks, video conferencing software, and interactive presentations, are essential for effectively communicating with clients and presenting properties in a compelling manner.

These tools help you convey information clearly, engage clients visually, and make a lasting impression during client meetings and property showings.

Training and Professional Development Programs: Continuous learning and professional development are essential for staying ahead in the real estate industry. Investing in training programs, workshops, and certifications can help you sharpen your skills, stay abreast of industry trends, and enhance your credibility as a real estate professional.

Networking and Referral Programs: Networking and referral programs are powerful tools for expanding your client base and generating leads. By cultivating relationships with other real estate professionals, industry partners, and past clients, you can tap into a steady stream of referrals and opportunities for collaboration.

Time Management and Productivity Tools: Time management and productivity tools help you maximize efficiency and prioritize tasks effectively. Whether it's a task management app, a calendar tool, or a time tracking software, these tools help you stay organized, focused, and on track to achieve your sales goals.

Negotiation and Sales Training Resources: Negotiation and sales training resources provide valuable insights and techniques for closing deals with confidence and finesse. Whether through books, online courses, or workshops, investing in your negotiation skills and sales acumen can significantly enhance your success as a real estate professional.

By leveraging these tools and techniques, you can build a robust sales arsenal that empowers you to excel in the competitive world of real estate sales. From managing client relationships and marketing properties to conducting market research and closing deals, each tool plays a crucial role in helping you achieve your sales goals and deliver exceptional results for your clients.

Effective Communication

"Effective Communication: The Heart of Real Estate Sales" is a cornerstone chapter within "Closing Deals and Opening Doors: A Practical Guide to Real Estate Sales." At its core, effective communication lies at the heart of successful real estate transactions. In this chapter, we delve into the intricacies of communication within the context of real estate sales, exploring the essential principles, strategies, and techniques that underpin meaningful client interactions and drive successful outcomes.

Clear and Transparent Communication forms the foundation of effective real estate sales. From the initial client consultation to the closing table, transparent communication fosters trust, builds rapport, and ensures that all parties are on the same page. This involves actively listening to clients' needs, concerns, and preferences, and articulating information clearly and concisely.

Empathy and Understanding are essential components of effective communication in real estate sales. By putting yourself in the client's shoes and understanding their perspective, you can better address their needs, alleviate concerns, and tailor your approach to meet their unique circumstances. Empathetic communication demonstrates your commitment to serving the client's best interests and fosters a deeper sense of trust and rapport.

Adaptability and Flexibility are crucial in navigating the diverse personalities and communication styles encountered in real estate sales. Effective communicators are adept at adjusting their approach to suit the preferences and preferences of each client, whether it's providing detailed market analysis to analytical clients or offering emotional support to those navigating significant life transitions.

Clarity and Conciseness are paramount in conveying information effectively in the fast-paced world of real estate sales. Whether explaining complex legal documents, outlining pricing strategies, or presenting property features, clear and concise communication ensures that clients understand the information presented and can make informed decisions with confidence.

Timeliness and Responsiveness are essential in maintaining open lines of communication throughout the sales process. Promptly responding to client inquiries, providing updates on listing activity, and addressing concerns in a timely manner demonstrate your commitment to client satisfaction and build trust and confidence in your abilities as a real estate professional.

Professionalism and Respect underpin all communication interactions in real estate sales. Treating clients, colleagues, and industry partners with professionalism, courtesy, and respect fosters positive relationships and enhances your reputation as a trusted and reliable real estate professional. Professional communication instills confidence in clients and sets the tone for successful transactions.

Conflict Resolution Skills are invaluable in navigating challenging situations and resolving conflicts that may arise during the sales process. Whether negotiating terms with other parties, addressing client concerns, or mediating disputes, effective communicators are skilled at finding mutually beneficial solutions and maintaining positive relationships throughout the transaction.

Technology and Communication Tools play an increasingly important role in real estate sales, facilitating communication with clients, marketing properties, and streamlining transactions. From email and text messaging to video conferencing and virtual tours, leveraging technology effectively enhances communication efficiency and expands your reach to a broader audience.

In summary, effective communication is the lifeblood of real estate sales, shaping client relationships, driving successful transactions, and fostering trust and confidence in your abilities as a real estate professional. By embracing principles of transparency, empathy, adaptability, and professionalism, and leveraging communication tools and techniques effectively, you can navigate the complexities of the sales process with clarity, conviction, and success.

The Psychology of Selling: Understanding Buyer Behavior

"The Psychology of Selling: Understanding Buyer Behavior" delves into the intricacies of human psychology and its profound influence on the real estate sales process. In this chapter, we explore the underlying motivations, biases, and decision-making processes that shape buyer behavior, equipping you with the insights and strategies needed to connect with clients on a deeper level and guide them toward successful transactions.

Understanding Emotional Drivers is paramount in real estate sales, as purchasing property is often a deeply emotional decision. By recognizing that buyers' decisions are driven by a combination of rational factors and emotional triggers, you can tailor your approach to address both practical needs and aspirational desires. Whether it's the desire for security, status, or a sense of belonging, tapping into buyers' emotions allows you to create meaningful connections and present properties in a compelling light.

Building Trust and Credibility is essential for gaining buyers' confidence and establishing yourself as a trusted advisor. Trust is cultivated through transparency, integrity, and consistency in your actions and communication. By demonstrating your expertise, providing honest advice, and delivering on promises, you instill confidence in buyers and position yourself as a reliable source of guidance throughout the purchasing process.

Addressing Pain Points and Overcoming Objections requires empathy and understanding of buyers' concerns and hesitations. Whether it's financial constraints, uncertainty about the market, or fears of making the wrong decision, effective sales professionals are skilled at identifying and addressing buyers' pain points with sensitivity and reassurance. By listening attentively, addressing concerns proactively, and providing relevant information and solutions, you can alleviate buyers' anxieties and build trust in your ability to guide them toward a successful purchase.

Utilizing Persuasion Techniques allows you to influence buyers' decisions and nudge them toward taking action. From the use of persuasive language and storytelling to the presentation of social proof and testimonials, persuasion techniques help you frame properties in a favorable light and highlight their value proposition. By appealing to buyers' logic, emotions, and social influences, you can motivate them to move forward with confidence and conviction.

Recognizing Cognitive Biases and Heuristics that influence buyer decision-making is essential for understanding how buyers process information and make choices. From the anchoring effect and confirmation bias to the scarcity heuristic and social proof, cognitive biases can shape buyers' perceptions and preferences in subtle ways. By being aware of these biases and adjusting your approach accordingly, you can present information in a way that resonates with buyers and helps them make informed decisions.

Creating a Positive Buying Experience goes beyond the transaction itself and encompasses the entire journey from initial contact to closing. By providing exceptional service, personalized attention, and a seamless experience, you enhance buyers' satisfaction and loyalty. Positive buying experiences not only lead to successful transactions but also generate referrals and repeat business, fueling your long-term success as a real estate professional.

In summary, understanding buyer behavior is a cornerstone of successful real estate sales. By delving into the psychology of selling, you gain valuable insights into buyers' motivations, concerns, and decision-making processes, allowing you to tailor your approach, build trust, and guide clients toward successful transactions with confidence and empathy.

Creating Compelling Listings

"Creating Compelling Listings: Strategies for Attracting Buyers" is a critical aspect of real estate sales, as it serves as the primary tool for showcasing properties and capturing the interest of potential buyers. In this chapter, we explore the strategies and techniques that enable you to craft listings that stand out in a competitive market and resonate with prospective buyers.

Captivating Headlines and Descriptions are essential for grabbing buyers' attention and enticing them to learn more about a property. A compelling headline should be concise, descriptive, and attention-grabbing, highlighting the property's most attractive features or unique selling points. Similarly, property descriptions should be informative, engaging, and tailored to the target audience, painting a vivid picture of the property and its lifestyle benefits.

High-Quality Photography is key to making a strong first impression and showcasing the property in its best light. Professional-quality photos that are well-lit, properly composed, and edited to enhance visual appeal can significantly impact buyers' perception of a property. Additionally, including a variety of photos that capture different angles, rooms, and features helps buyers envision themselves living in the space.

Virtual Tours and Video Walkthroughs offer immersive experiences that allow buyers to explore properties from the comfort of their own homes. By providing virtual tours or video walkthroughs, you give buyers a comprehensive view of the property's layout, flow, and amenities, enhancing their understanding and interest in the listing. These visual tools are particularly valuable for attracting out-of-town buyers or those unable to attend in-person showings.

Highlighting Key Features and Benefits helps buyers quickly assess whether a property meets their needs and preferences. Clearly identifying and showcasing the property's standout features, such as upgraded appliances, outdoor living spaces, or proximity to amenities, allows buyers to easily discern the value proposition and benefits of the property.

Including Floor Plans and Property Details adds depth and transparency to your listings, providing buyers with essential information to make informed decisions. Floor plans help buyers visualize the property's layout and flow, while detailed property descriptions that outline specifications, dimensions, and amenities provide clarity and reduce ambiguity.

Utilizing Compelling Visuals and Graphics enhances the appeal of your listings and reinforces key selling points. Incorporating high-quality images, infographics, and interactive elements can make your listings more visually engaging and memorable. Additionally, staging photos with tasteful decor and furnishings can help buyers envision the potential of the space and imagine themselves living there.

Optimizing for Search Engines and Online Platforms ensures that your listings reach a wider audience and appear prominently in search results. By incorporating relevant keywords, descriptive phrases, and location-based tags into your listings, you increase their visibility and attract more qualified leads. Additionally, leveraging multiple online platforms and real estate websites expands your reach and exposure to potential buyers.

Engaging and Responsive Communication is essential for converting interest into action. Promptly responding to inquiries, providing additional information, and scheduling showings in a timely manner demonstrate your responsiveness and commitment to customer service. By maintaining open lines of communication and being readily available to address buyers' questions and concerns, you foster trust and confidence in your professionalism.

In summary, creating compelling listings requires a strategic approach that combines visual appeal, informative content, and effective communication. By implementing these strategies and techniques, you can attract buyers' attention, generate interest in your listings, and ultimately, facilitate successful transactions in the real estate market.

The Open House Advantage

"The Open House Advantage: Showcasing Properties for Maximum Impact" is a pivotal chapter within "Closing Deals and Opening Doors: A Practical Guide to Real Estate Sales." Open houses serve as powerful opportunities to showcase properties to potential buyers in a dynamic and interactive setting. In this chapter, we explore the strategies and techniques that enable you to leverage the open house advantage and maximize the impact of property showings.

Strategic Planning is essential for hosting successful open houses that attract qualified buyers and generate excitement about the property. This involves setting clear objectives, identifying target demographics, and scheduling the open house at times when foot traffic is likely to be highest. By strategically planning the event, you can maximize attendance and create a buzz around the property.

Creating a Welcoming Atmosphere sets the stage for a positive open house experience. From curb appeal to interior staging, every aspect of the property should be meticulously prepared to make a favorable impression on visitors. Clean, clutter-free spaces, inviting decor, and pleasant aromas enhance the ambiance and make prospective buyers feel welcome and at ease.

Highlighting Key Features and Amenities allows you to showcase the property's most attractive attributes and differentiate it from competing listings. Whether it's a gourmet kitchen, luxurious master suite, or stunning outdoor living space, emphasizing standout features captures buyers' attention and piques their interest in the property.

Offering Refreshments and Snacks adds a thoughtful touch to the open house experience and encourages visitors to linger longer. Providing light refreshments such as water, coffee, or snacks creates a hospitable atmosphere and encourages conversation among attendees. Additionally, branded promotional items or informational materials can serve as memorable takeaways that keep your brand top-of-mind with potential buyers.

Engaging Attendees through Interactive Activities and Demonstrations enhances the open house experience and fosters deeper connections with prospective buyers. Whether it's hosting a cooking demonstration in the kitchen, showcasing smart home features, or offering guided tours of the property, interactive activities create memorable moments and help buyers envision themselves living in the space.

Utilizing Technology and Digital Tools enhances the effectiveness of open houses and extends your reach to a broader audience. Virtual tours, 3D walkthroughs, and interactive floor plans allow remote buyers to explore the property from anywhere in the world. Additionally, leveraging social media platforms and online marketing channels helps promote the open house and attract more attendees.

Encouraging Feedback and Follow-Up is essential for gathering valuable insights and maintaining momentum after the open house. Collecting feedback from attendees allows you to identify areas for improvement and tailor your approach for future events. Following up with interested buyers, providing additional information, and scheduling private showings demonstrate your responsiveness and commitment to helping them find their dream home.

In summary, the open house advantage provides a unique opportunity to showcase properties to potential buyers in a compelling and engaging manner. By implementing strategic planning, creating a welcoming atmosphere, highlighting key features, and leveraging technology, you can maximize the impact of your open houses and drive successful outcomes in the real estate market.

Negotiation Skills: Closing Deals with Confidence

"Negotiation Skills: Closing Deals with Confidence" is a crucial chapter within "Closing Deals and Opening Doors: A Practical Guide to Real Estate Sales." Effective negotiation skills are essential for navigating the complexities of real estate transactions, resolving conflicts, and ultimately, closing deals with confidence. In this chapter, we delve into the necessary negotiation skills and strategies that enable you to achieve successful outcomes in the competitive real estate market.

Preparation and Planning: Successful negotiations begin long before sitting down at the bargaining table. This involves thorough preparation, including researching market trends, understanding the property's value, and identifying your client's priorities and goals. By arming yourself with relevant information and a clear understanding of the negotiation dynamics, you can enter negotiations with confidence and clarity.

Active Listening: Active listening is a fundamental negotiation skill that involves fully understanding the other party's perspective, interests, and concerns. By listening attentively and empathetically to the other party's needs and motivations, you can identify common ground, uncover underlying interests, and build rapport, paving the way for more constructive and collaborative negotiations.

Effective Communication: Effective communication is essential for conveying your interests, articulating your position, and advocating for your client's needs during negotiations. Clear and concise communication helps prevent misunderstandings, fosters mutual understanding, and enhances the likelihood of reaching mutually beneficial agreements. Additionally, being assertive while maintaining professionalism is key to advocating for your client's interests with confidence and conviction.

Creative Problem-Solving: Negotiation often involves finding creative solutions to overcome obstacles and address conflicting interests. Creative problem-solving skills allow you to think outside the box, explore alternative options, and generate win-win solutions that satisfy both parties' needs. By adopting a collaborative mindset and focusing on shared interests, you can break through impasses and reach agreements that maximize value for all involved.

Emotional Intelligence: Emotional intelligence plays a crucial role in negotiation, as emotions can significantly influence decision-making and behavior. By remaining calm, composed, and empathetic, even in the face of challenging situations, you can navigate negotiations more effectively and build trust with the other party. Additionally, being able to manage your emotions and recognize and respond to the emotions of others helps foster constructive dialogue and maintain positive rapport throughout the negotiation process.

Flexibility and Adaptability: Negotiation is a dynamic process that requires flexibility and adaptability to respond to changing circumstances and unexpected developments. Being willing to adjust your approach, explore new options, and make concessions when necessary can help keep negotiations moving forward and increase the likelihood of reaching a successful outcome. However, it's important to maintain a clear understanding of your client's priorities and boundaries to ensure that any concessions made are in their best interests.

Strategic Thinking: Strategic thinking is essential for anticipating the other party's moves, identifying potential areas of agreement or contention, and formulating a negotiation strategy that aligns with your client's objectives. By thinking strategically and considering the long-term implications of different negotiation outcomes, you can position yourself to achieve the best possible result for your client.

Closing the Deal: Closing the deal requires finesse and assertiveness to finalize the terms and reach a mutually acceptable agreement. This may involve clarifying any remaining points of contention, addressing last-minute concerns, and ensuring that all parties are satisfied with the terms before signing the agreement. By confidently guiding the negotiation to a successful conclusion, you demonstrate your value as a skilled negotiator and trusted advocate for your client.

In summary, negotiation skills are essential for navigating the complexities of real estate transactions and achieving successful outcomes for your clients. By mastering the necessary negotiation skills and strategies outlined in this chapter, you can approach negotiations with confidence, advocate effectively for your client's interests, and close deals that satisfy all parties involved.

Handling Objections: Turning Challenges into Opportunities

"Handling Objections: Turning Challenges into Opportunities" is a critical chapter within "Closing Deals and Opening Doors: A Practical Guide to Real Estate Sales." Objections are inevitable in the real estate sales process and are often perceived as obstacles to overcome. However, skilled sales professionals understand that objections can be reframed as opportunities to address concerns, build trust, and ultimately, move the sales process forward. In this chapter, we explore the strategies and techniques for effectively handling objections and turning them into opportunities for success.

Anticipating Common Objections: The first step in handling objections is to anticipate and prepare for common concerns that buyers or sellers may raise. These objections could relate to pricing, property condition, location, market conditions, or personal preferences. By identifying potential objections in advance, you can develop thoughtful responses and address concerns proactively during the sales process.

Active Listening and Empathy: When faced with objections, it's essential to listen attentively to the other party's concerns and empathize with their perspective. Active listening demonstrates respect for the other party's opinions and allows you to gain a deeper understanding of their underlying motivations and interests. By acknowledging their concerns and validating their feelings, you can build rapport and create a more conducive environment for constructive dialogue.

Clarifying and Addressing Concerns: Once objections are raised, it's important to clarify and address them directly, providing accurate information and reassurance where needed. This may involve educating clients about market trends, providing data to support pricing decisions, or offering solutions to address property-related concerns. By addressing objections openly and transparently, you can build trust and credibility with clients and alleviate their concerns.

Highlighting Benefits and Value Proposition: One effective strategy for handling objections is to highlight the benefits and value proposition of the property or service being offered. By focusing on the unique features, advantages, and lifestyle benefits that the property provides, you can shift the conversation from objections to opportunities. Emphasizing the value proposition helps buyers or sellers see the potential upside and overcome their reservations.

Offering Alternatives and Solutions: In some cases, objections may stem from specific preferences or requirements that can't be met with the current offering. In such situations, offering alternatives or creative solutions can help address clients' needs and keep the conversation moving forward. Whether it's suggesting alternative properties, adjusting pricing or terms, or exploring different strategies, offering solutions demonstrates flexibility and a commitment to finding mutually beneficial outcomes.

Building Trust and Credibility: Trust is essential in overcoming objections and fostering confidence in the sales process. By consistently demonstrating honesty, integrity, and professionalism, you can build trust and credibility with clients, making them more receptive to your recommendations and more willing to overcome objections. Trust is the foundation of successful relationships in real estate sales and is essential for turning objections into opportunities.

Closing with Confidence: Once objections have been addressed satisfactorily, it's important to close the conversation with confidence and conviction. Reiterate the key benefits and value proposition, summarize the agreed-upon solutions, and invite the other party to take the next step in the sales process. By closing with confidence and enthusiasm, you reinforce the positive aspects of the discussion and encourage clients to move forward with the transaction.

In summary, handling objections is an essential skill in real estate sales, requiring active listening, empathy, and problem-solving abilities. By reframing objections as opportunities to address concerns, build trust, and demonstrate value, you can turn challenges into opportunities for success in the sales process. With preparation, empathy, and a commitment to building trust, skilled sales professionals can navigate objections effectively and achieve positive outcomes for their clients.

Technology in Sales: Leveraging Digital Tools for Efficiency

"Technology in Sales: Leveraging Digital Tools for Efficiency" is a pivotal chapter within "Closing Deals and Opening Doors: A Practical Guide to Real Estate Sales." In today's digital age, technology plays a central role in enhancing efficiency, streamlining processes, and maximizing productivity in real estate sales. In this chapter, we explore the wide range of digital tools and technologies available to real estate professionals and how they can be leveraged to drive success in sales.

Customer Relationship Management (CRM) Systems: CRM systems are powerful tools for managing client relationships, organizing leads, and tracking interactions throughout the sales process. By centralizing client data, communication history, and transaction details in a single platform, CRM systems enable real estate professionals to stay organized, nurture leads effectively, and provide personalized service to clients.

Listing Management Software: Listing management software simplifies the process of creating, updating, and promoting property listings across multiple platforms. These tools allow real estate professionals to input property details, upload photos and videos, and syndicate listings to various websites and listing portals with ease. By automating listing management tasks, real estate professionals can save time and ensure that properties reach a wider audience.

Virtual Tour and 3D Imaging Technology: Virtual tour and 3D imaging technology allow potential buyers to explore properties remotely in immersive detail. By offering virtual tours and 3D walkthroughs, real estate professionals can provide prospective buyers with a realistic sense of the property's layout, features, and amenities, without the need for an in-person visit. This technology enhances the buyer experience, attracts more qualified leads, and accelerates the sales process.

Digital Marketing Platforms: Digital marketing platforms, such as social media, email marketing, and online advertising, offer powerful channels for reaching and engaging with potential buyers. Real estate professionals can leverage these platforms to promote listings, showcase properties, and nurture leads through targeted advertising, content marketing, and email campaigns. Digital marketing platforms enable real estate professionals to expand their reach, generate leads, and build brand awareness in a cost-effective manner.

Document Management Systems: Document management systems streamline the process of creating, editing, and storing transaction documents electronically. These systems allow real estate professionals to securely manage contracts, disclosures, and other legal documents, reducing paperwork, minimizing errors, and improving compliance. Document management systems also facilitate collaboration with clients, lenders, and other stakeholders, enabling real-time document sharing and electronic signatures.

Mobile Apps and Communication Tools: Mobile apps and communication tools enable real estate professionals to stay connected and productive while on the go. Whether it's accessing property listings, communicating with clients, or scheduling appointments, mobile apps provide real-time access to essential information and tools from any location. Additionally, communication tools such as video conferencing, messaging apps, and virtual meeting platforms facilitate remote collaboration and client communication, enhancing efficiency and flexibility in the sales process.

Data Analytics and Market Research Tools: Data analytics and market research tools provide valuable insights into market trends, pricing dynamics, and consumer behavior. Real estate professionals can leverage these tools to analyze housing market data, identify emerging trends, and make data-driven decisions about pricing, marketing, and investment opportunities. By staying informed about market conditions and consumer preferences, real estate professionals can adapt their strategies and stay ahead of the competition.

Transaction Management Platforms: Transaction management platforms streamline the process of managing real estate transactions from start to finish. These platforms offer features such as task tracking, document storage, and transaction coordination, allowing real estate professionals to manage multiple transactions efficiently and ensure that deadlines are met. Transaction management platforms centralize transaction-related information and communication, reducing administrative burden and improving collaboration with clients and other stakeholders.

In summary, technology plays a transformative role in real estate sales, enabling real estate professionals to work more efficiently, attract more qualified leads, and provide a better experience for clients. By leveraging digital tools and technologies effectively, real estate professionals can streamline processes, enhance productivity, and ultimately, achieve greater success in sales.

Networking and Relationship Building

"Networking and Relationship Building: Opening Doors to Opportunities" underscores the fundamental role of interpersonal connections in the realm of real estate sales. In this chapter, we explore the significance of networking and relationship building, and how they serve as catalysts for unlocking opportunities and driving success in the industry.

Building a Strong Professional Network: A robust professional network is the cornerstone of success in real estate sales. Networking involves cultivating relationships with other industry professionals, including fellow real estate agents, brokers, lenders, attorneys, contractors, and service providers. By actively participating in industry events, joining professional organizations, and engaging in networking activities, real estate professionals can expand their network, exchange valuable insights, and access a wealth of resources and opportunities.

Establishing Trust and Credibility: Trust and credibility are essential for building lasting relationships in real estate sales. Real estate professionals must demonstrate integrity, honesty, and reliability in their interactions with clients and industry peers. By consistently delivering on promises, providing exceptional service, and acting with professionalism, real estate professionals earn the trust and respect of others, laying the foundation for fruitful collaborations and referrals.

Effective Communication and Engagement: Effective communication is key to nurturing relationships and staying top-of-mind with clients and industry contacts. Real estate professionals should maintain open lines of communication, actively listen to others' needs and preferences, and provide timely and relevant information. Whether it's following up with clients, sharing market insights, or offering assistance to colleagues, consistent and meaningful communication fosters stronger connections and reinforces trust.

Offering Value and Support: Providing value and support to others is essential for building meaningful relationships in real estate sales. Real estate professionals can offer assistance, guidance, and expertise to clients and industry contacts, whether it's helping clients navigate the buying or selling process, providing market updates, or offering referrals to trusted service providers. By demonstrating a genuine desire to help others succeed, real estate professionals can build goodwill and loyalty, leading to long-term relationships and repeat business.

Staying Visible and Engaged: Staying visible and engaged within the industry is crucial for maintaining and expanding your network. Real estate professionals should actively participate in networking events, industry conferences, and community activities to stay connected with peers and potential clients. Additionally, leveraging online platforms such as social media, professional networking sites, and industry forums can help real estate professionals expand their reach and visibility within the industry.

Investing in Relationship Building: Relationship building is an ongoing process that requires time, effort, and investment. Real estate professionals should prioritize relationship building as a core aspect of their business strategy, dedicating time to nurture existing connections and cultivate new ones. This may involve scheduling regular meetings or coffee chats with clients and industry contacts, sending personalized notes or gifts to show appreciation, and proactively seeking opportunities to add value and support others.

Harnessing the Power of Referrals and Recommendations: Referrals and recommendations are powerful tools for expanding your network and attracting new business in real estate sales. Satisfied clients and satisfied industry contacts are more likely to refer others to you and recommend your services based on their positive experiences. Real estate professionals should actively seek referrals and recommendations from satisfied clients and colleagues, and reciprocate by referring business to others whenever possible.

In summary, networking and relationship building are essential components of success in real estate sales. By investing in building strong professional networks, establishing trust and credibility, offering value and support, staying visible and engaged, and harnessing the power of referrals and recommendations, real estate professionals can open doors to new opportunities, drive business growth, and achieve long-term success in the industry.

Marketing Mastery

"Marketing Mastery: Promoting Properties for Quick Sales" delves into the art and science of effectively marketing properties to attract qualified buyers and expedite the sales process. In this chapter, we explore the strategies and techniques that real estate professionals can employ to master the marketing game and achieve swift sales.

Comprehensive Market Analysis: Before diving into marketing efforts, it's essential to conduct a comprehensive market analysis to understand current market conditions, trends, and buyer preferences. By analyzing comparable sales, assessing demand-supply dynamics, and identifying target demographics, real estate professionals can tailor their marketing strategies to maximize effectiveness and appeal to the right audience.

Strategic Pricing: Pricing plays a pivotal role in the success of any marketing campaign. Real estate professionals should strategically price properties based on market conditions, comparable sales, and property features to attract buyers and generate interest. Pricing properties competitively from the outset can create a sense of urgency among buyers and increase the likelihood of a quick sale.

Professional Photography and Staging: High-quality photography and staging are essential for capturing buyers' attention and making a strong first impression. Professional photographers can highlight the property's best features and showcase it in the best possible light, while staging experts can enhance its visual appeal and help buyers envision themselves living in the space. Investing in professional photography and staging pays dividends by attracting more qualified buyers and accelerating the sales process.

Compelling Property Descriptions: Compelling property descriptions are key to engaging potential buyers and piquing their interest. Real estate professionals should craft descriptive, enticing narratives that highlight the property's unique features, amenities, and lifestyle benefits. By telling a compelling story and painting a vivid picture of the property, real estate professionals can captivate buyers' imaginations and motivate them to take action.

Multi-Channel Marketing: Effective marketing requires reaching buyers where they are and engaging them through multiple channels. Real estate professionals should leverage a mix of traditional and digital marketing channels, including online listings, social media platforms, email marketing, print advertising, and signage. By casting a wide net and reaching buyers across various channels, real estate professionals can maximize exposure and attract more potential buyers to the property.

Targeted Advertising Campaigns: Targeted advertising campaigns allow real estate professionals to reach specific demographics and audience segments with tailored messaging. By leveraging demographic data, behavioral insights, and geotargeting capabilities, real estate professionals can create targeted advertising campaigns that resonate with the right audience and drive qualified leads to the property. Whether it's through online advertising platforms, social media ads, or local publications, targeted advertising helps real estate professionals reach buyers effectively and efficiently.

Open Houses and Events: Open houses and events provide valuable opportunities to showcase properties to potential buyers in a personalized and interactive setting. Real estate professionals can host open houses, broker tours, or themed events to attract buyers, generate buzz, and facilitate face-to-face interactions. By creating a memorable experience and engaging with buyers directly, real estate professionals can forge connections, answer questions, and address concerns, ultimately driving faster sales.

Follow-Up and Persistence: Following up with leads and maintaining consistent communication is crucial for converting interest into action. Real estate professionals should promptly follow up with interested buyers, provide additional information, and schedule property showings to keep the momentum going. By staying proactive, responsive, and persistent, real estate professionals can nurture leads, overcome objections, and ultimately, close deals more quickly.

In summary, mastering the art of marketing is essential for promoting properties effectively and achieving quick sales in the real estate market. By employing strategic pricing, professional photography and staging, compelling property descriptions, multi-channel marketing, targeted advertising campaigns, open houses and events, and diligent follow-up, real estate professionals can create a winning marketing strategy that attracts qualified buyers and accelerates the sales process.

Time Management for Sales Professionals

"Time Management for Sales Professionals: Maximizing Productivity" is a critical component of success in the fast-paced world of real estate sales. In this chapter, we explore the strategies and techniques that sales professionals can employ to manage their time effectively, prioritize tasks, and maximize productivity in their daily activities.

Prioritize Tasks: Effective time management begins with prioritizing tasks based on their importance and urgency. Sales professionals should identify high-priority activities, such as prospecting, client meetings, and contract negotiations, and allocate sufficient time and resources to these tasks. By focusing on activities that directly contribute to sales and revenue generation, sales professionals can make the most of their time and achieve meaningful results.

Set Clear Goals and Objectives: Setting clear goals and objectives provides a roadmap for prioritizing tasks and staying focused on what matters most. Sales professionals should establish specific, measurable, and achievable goals for sales targets, client acquisition, and business growth. By breaking down larger goals into smaller, actionable steps, sales professionals can track progress, stay motivated, and maintain momentum toward achieving their objectives.

Create a Daily Schedule: Creating a daily schedule helps sales professionals organize their time effectively and stay on track with their tasks and activities. Sales professionals should block out dedicated time slots for key activities such as prospecting, client meetings, follow-up calls, and administrative tasks. By adhering to a structured schedule, sales professionals can minimize distractions, maintain focus, and make the most of their productive hours.

Utilize Time Blocking Techniques: Time blocking involves allocating specific time blocks for different tasks or activities throughout the day. Sales professionals can designate uninterrupted blocks of time for focused work, such as prospecting or proposal preparation, and set aside time for meetings, calls, and email correspondence. By batching similar tasks together and minimizing context switching, sales professionals can optimize their productivity and efficiency.

Delegate and Automate Routine Tasks: Delegating and automating routine tasks can free up valuable time and mental bandwidth for sales professionals to focus on higher-value activities. Sales professionals should identify tasks that can be delegated to support staff or automated using technology solutions such as email automation, task management tools, and customer relationship management (CRM) systems. By leveraging delegation and automation, sales professionals can streamline their workflows and increase their capacity to handle more complex and strategic tasks.

Limit Distractions: Distractions can derail productivity and impede progress toward goals. Sales professionals should identify common sources of distraction, such as email, social media, or unnecessary meetings, and implement strategies to minimize their impact. This may involve setting boundaries around email and phone usage, designating specific times for checking messages, and creating a distraction-free work environment. By maintaining focus and minimizing interruptions, sales professionals can optimize their productivity and accomplish more in less time.

Take Regular Breaks: Taking regular breaks is essential for maintaining energy, focus, and productivity throughout the day. Sales professionals should schedule short breaks between tasks or activities to rest, recharge, and rejuvenate. Whether it's taking a walk, practicing mindfulness, or enjoying a healthy snack, breaks allow sales professionals to reset their mental state, alleviate stress, and return to work with renewed focus and productivity.

Review and Reflect: Regularly reviewing and reflecting on time management practices allows sales professionals to identify areas for improvement and make adjustments as needed. Sales professionals should periodically evaluate their daily routines, productivity habits, and time allocation strategies to identify inefficiencies or bottlenecks. By learning from past experiences and making proactive changes, sales professionals can continuously optimize their time management practices and maximize productivity over the long term.

In summary, mastering time management is essential for sales professionals to maximize productivity, achieve their goals, and succeed in the competitive world of real estate sales. By prioritizing tasks, setting clear goals, creating a structured schedule, utilizing time blocking techniques, delegating and automating routine tasks, limiting distractions, taking regular breaks, and reviewing and reflecting on their time management practices, sales professionals can optimize their efficiency and effectiveness in managing their time and accomplishing their objectives.

The Closing Process: Sealing the Deal with Precision

"The Closing Process: Sealing the Deal with Precision" marks the culmination of the real estate sales journey, where all the groundwork and negotiations converge into a final agreement. In this chapter, we explore the essential steps and strategies involved in the closing process to ensure a smooth and successful transaction.

Finalizing Terms and Conditions: The closing process begins with finalizing the terms and conditions of the sale. This includes reviewing the purchase agreement, addressing any contingencies or conditions, and clarifying details such as price, financing, and closing date. Real estate professionals play a crucial role in facilitating communication between buyers and sellers, ensuring that all parties are in agreement before proceeding to closing.

Completing Due Diligence: Before closing, both buyers and sellers typically conduct due diligence to verify the property's condition and ensure that all legal and financial aspects are in order. Buyers may conduct inspections, review property disclosures, and confirm financing arrangements, while sellers may provide additional documentation such as title reports or property surveys. Real estate professionals assist their clients in navigating this process, coordinating inspections, and addressing any issues that arise.

Securing Financing: For most buyers, securing financing is a critical aspect of the closing process. This involves finalizing mortgage approval, coordinating with lenders, and ensuring that all necessary documents are in order. Real estate professionals work closely with buyers and lenders to facilitate the financing process, providing guidance and support to ensure a seamless transition to closing.

Preparing Closing Documents: As the closing date approaches, various legal and financial documents must be prepared and signed by both parties. These may include the closing statement, deed of trust, loan documents, and transfer of ownership forms. Real estate professionals play a crucial role in preparing and reviewing these documents, ensuring accuracy and compliance with applicable laws and regulations.

Conducting the Closing Meeting: The closing meeting is the final step in the process, where buyers and sellers come together to sign the necessary documents and transfer ownership of the property. Real estate professionals often coordinate the closing meeting, ensuring that all parties are present and facilitating the signing of documents. They may also answer any remaining questions and provide guidance throughout the process.

Facilitating Fund Transfer and Title Transfer: During the closing meeting, funds are transferred from the buyer to the seller, typically through an escrow or closing agent. Additionally, the title to the property is transferred from the seller to the buyer, completing the sale transaction. Real estate professionals oversee these transactions, ensuring that all funds are transferred securely and that the title transfer process is completed according to legal requirements.

Addressing Last-Minute Issues: Despite careful planning, last-minute issues or challenges may arise during the closing process. Real estate professionals are trained to anticipate and address these issues quickly and effectively, minimizing disruptions and ensuring that the closing proceeds smoothly. Whether it's resolving outstanding liens, addressing financing delays, or coordinating with third-party vendors, real estate professionals act as advocates for their clients, advocating for their best interests and ensuring a successful closing.

Celebrating the Successful Closing: Once all documents are signed, funds are transferred, and ownership is transferred, the sale transaction is officially closed. Real estate professionals congratulate their clients on a successful closing and celebrate the achievement of their real estate goals. They may also provide guidance on next steps, such as transferring utilities or obtaining keys, to ensure a smooth transition for buyers and sellers.

In summary, the closing process is a critical phase in the real estate sales journey, requiring careful coordination, attention to detail, and effective communication. By following these essential steps and strategies, real estate professionals can ensure a smooth and successful closing, sealing the deal with precision and delivering a positive experience for their clients.

Post-Sale Service: Building Client Loyalty and Referrals

"Post-Sale Service: Building Client Loyalty and Referrals" is a crucial aspect of real estate sales that extends beyond the closing of a transaction. In this chapter, we explore the importance of providing exceptional post-sale service to clients and strategies for fostering long-term relationships that lead to client loyalty and referrals.

Delivering Exceptional Customer Service: Providing exceptional customer service is the foundation of building client loyalty and generating referrals. Real estate professionals should continue to prioritize their clients' needs even after the sale is closed. This involves being responsive to inquiries, addressing any post-sale concerns or issues promptly, and going above and beyond to ensure client satisfaction. By demonstrating a commitment to delivering outstanding service, real estate professionals can earn their clients' trust and loyalty.

Maintaining Regular Communication: Regular communication is key to staying connected with clients and maintaining a strong relationship over time. Real estate professionals should stay in touch with past clients through periodic check-ins, newsletters, or personalized emails. By providing valuable market updates, tips on home maintenance, or information on local events and resources, real estate professionals can continue to add value to their clients' lives long after the transaction is complete.

Offering Ongoing Support and Resources: Clients may have ongoing real estate needs or questions even after the sale is finalized. Real estate professionals can offer ongoing support and resources to assist clients with their evolving needs. Whether it's providing recommendations for local contractors, offering guidance on property taxes or homeownership issues, or connecting clients with trusted service providers, real estate professionals can position themselves as trusted advisors and valuable resources for their clients.

Soliciting Feedback and Reviews: Soliciting feedback and reviews from clients is a valuable way to gauge satisfaction and identify areas for improvement. Real estate professionals should actively seek feedback from clients after the sale is closed, asking about their experience and whether there are any areas where service could be improved. Positive reviews and testimonials from satisfied clients can also serve as powerful marketing tools, helping to build credibility and attract new business through word-of-mouth referrals.

Providing Value-Added Services: Real estate professionals can differentiate themselves and enhance client loyalty by offering value-added services beyond the transaction. This may include hosting client appreciation events, providing educational workshops or seminars, or offering exclusive discounts or incentives for past clients. By demonstrating a commitment to adding value and supporting their clients' ongoing needs, real estate professionals can strengthen their relationships and foster loyalty over the long term.

Creating a Referral Program: Referrals are a powerful source of new business in the real estate industry. Real estate professionals can create a referral program to incentivize past clients to refer their friends, family, and colleagues. This may involve offering rewards such as gift cards, discounts on future services, or even charitable donations in clients' names. By rewarding clients for their referrals, real estate professionals can encourage them to become brand ambassadors and advocates for their business.

Nurturing Long-Term Relationships: Building client loyalty and generating referrals is ultimately about nurturing long-term relationships based on trust, respect, and mutual benefit. Real estate professionals should view each client relationship as a long-term partnership and invest in building strong connections over time. By consistently delivering exceptional service, staying in touch, and providing ongoing support, real estate professionals can cultivate lasting relationships that lead to repeat business and referrals for years to come.

In summary, post-sale service is a critical component of real estate sales that can have a significant impact on client loyalty and referrals. By delivering exceptional customer service, maintaining regular communication, offering ongoing support and resources, soliciting feedback and reviews, providing value-added services, creating a referral program, and nurturing long-term relationships, real estate professionals can build strong connections with their clients and position themselves for continued success in the industry.

Growing Your Real Estate Sales Career

"Growing Your Real Estate Sales Career: Strategies for Long-Term Success" focuses on the continuous development and advancement of real estate professionals in their careers. In this chapter, we explore key strategies and approaches for achieving long-term success and fulfillment in the dynamic and competitive field of real estate sales.

Commit to Lifelong Learning: Real estate is an ever-evolving industry, with trends, regulations, and technologies constantly changing. To stay ahead of the curve and remain competitive, real estate professionals must commit to lifelong learning. This involves staying updated on industry developments, attending training sessions, earning certifications, and pursuing continuing education opportunities. By investing in their knowledge and skills, real estate professionals can adapt to changes in the market and position themselves as trusted experts in their field.

Set Clear Goals and Objectives: Setting clear, measurable goals is essential for guiding and motivating career growth in real estate sales. Real estate professionals should establish both short-term and long-term goals for sales targets, professional development, and personal growth. By defining specific objectives and creating actionable plans to achieve them, real estate professionals can stay focused and track their progress over time.

Develop a Niche or Specialization: Specializing in a particular niche or market segment can help real estate professionals stand out from the competition and attract clients with specific needs. Whether it's luxury properties, commercial real estate, investment properties, or niche markets such as seniors or first-time homebuyers, developing expertise in a specialized area allows real estate professionals to position themselves as go-to experts and command higher commissions.

Build a Strong Personal Brand: In today's digital age, personal branding is essential for establishing credibility, visibility, and trust in the real estate industry. Real estate professionals should invest in building a strong personal brand across online and offline channels, including websites, social media profiles, business cards, and professional networking events. By showcasing their expertise, values, and unique selling propositions, real estate professionals can attract clients and opportunities that align with their brand image.

Cultivate a Strong Professional Network: Networking is a powerful tool for expanding opportunities, gaining referrals, and building relationships in the real estate industry. Real estate professionals should actively cultivate and nurture their professional network by attending industry events, joining professional organizations, and participating in networking groups. By building relationships with fellow real estate professionals, industry influencers, and potential clients, real estate professionals can tap into valuable resources and opportunities for career growth.

Embrace Technology and Innovation: Technology has transformed the way real estate professionals conduct business, from marketing properties to communicating with clients to managing transactions. Real estate professionals should embrace technology and innovation to streamline processes, enhance efficiency, and deliver a superior client experience. This may involve leveraging digital marketing tools, adopting customer relationship management (CRM) systems, or using virtual reality and 3D imaging technology to showcase properties. By staying abreast of the latest technological advancements, real estate professionals can stay competitive and provide added value to their clients.

Provide Exceptional Client Service: Exceptional client service is the cornerstone of success in real estate sales. Real estate professionals should prioritize their clients' needs, communicate transparently, and go above and beyond to exceed expectations. By delivering outstanding service and creating memorable experiences for their clients, real estate professionals can earn their trust, loyalty, and referrals, paving the way for long-term success and growth in their careers.

Seek Mentorship and Guidance: Mentorship can be invaluable for real estate professionals seeking to accelerate their career growth and overcome challenges. Experienced mentors can provide guidance, support, and wisdom based on their own experiences in the industry. Real estate professionals should seek out mentorship opportunities and be open to learning from seasoned professionals who can offer insights, advice, and encouragement along their career journey.

In summary, growing a successful real estate sales career requires a combination of dedication, strategy, and continuous improvement. By committing to lifelong learning, setting clear goals, developing a niche, building a strong personal brand, cultivating a professional network, embracing technology, providing exceptional client service, and seeking mentorship, real estate professionals can position themselves for long-term success and fulfillment in their careers.

Final thought

In conclusion, "Closing Deals and Opening Doors: A Practical Guide to Real Estate Sales" has provided an in-depth exploration of the multifaceted world of real estate sales, offering valuable insights, strategies, and techniques for success. Throughout this comprehensive guide, we have delved into the art and science of real estate sales, from understanding market dynamics to mastering negotiation skills, and from leveraging technology to building lasting client relationships.

As real estate professionals, we understand that success in this dynamic industry requires more than just closing deals; it demands a commitment to excellence, continuous learning, and a dedication to providing exceptional service to clients. By embracing the principles and strategies outlined in this book, real estate professionals can navigate the complexities of the sales process with confidence, professionalism, and integrity.

We have explored the importance of effective communication, the psychology of selling, and the power of networking in building trust and rapport with clients. We have discussed the significance of marketing mastery, time management, and post-sale service in fostering long-term relationships and generating referrals. We have emphasized the importance of setting clear goals, embracing innovation, and cultivating a strong personal brand to achieve success in the competitive real estate market.

As we embark on our real estate sales careers, let us remember that our success is not measured solely by the number of transactions closed, but by the relationships we build, the trust we earn, and the positive impact we make on the lives of our clients. Let us continue to strive for excellence, to embrace change and innovation, and to always put the needs of our clients first.

In closing, "Closing Deals and Opening Doors" serves as a comprehensive resource and guide for real estate professionals at all stages of their careers. May the insights and strategies shared in this book inspire and empower you to achieve your goals, build a thriving real estate sales business, and make a lasting impact in the world of real estate.

www.ingramcontent.com/pod-product-compliance
Lightning Source LLC
Chambersburg PA
CBHW071213240526
45470CB00018B/1858